MRS HONEY'S LIST

Written by Sally Farrell Odgers
Illustrated by Jean Cooper-Brown

NON-TOXIC
Paint
Red
P.V.A. GLUE
GLUE
SCISS
PAPER

“What can you bring for the school fair?” asked Mrs Honey. “I want to make a list.”

“I can make a sponge cake,” said Emma. “A sponge cake with pink icing. That’s what I like best.”

Mrs Honey wrote it down.

"I can make cookies," said Tom.
"In lots of shapes.
That's what I like best."

Mrs Honey wrote it down.

"I can make chocolate brownies," said Jim.
"With coconut on top.
That's what I like best."

Mrs Honey wrote it down.

“I can make jam doughnuts,” said Jo.
“With strawberry jam.
That’s what I like best.”

Mrs Honey wrote it down.

"I can make little pies," said Cass.
"Apple pies. That's what I like best."

Mrs Honey wrote it down.

"I can make toffee," said Kim.
"With hundreds and thousands.
That's what I like best."

Mrs Honey wrote it down.

"That's very good," said Mrs Honey,
and she read her list aloud.

"The school fair is tomorrow,
so you will need to make everything tonight."

So Emma, Tom, Jim, Jo, Cass, and Kim
went home to make what they liked best.

"Have you all brought your food for the school fair?" asked Mrs Honey, next morning.

"Yes," they said.

Mrs Honey read out the list.

cake
toffee

Emma put up her hand.
"I couldn't make a sponge cake," she said,
"because we didn't have any eggs.
I made toffee instead."

Mrs Honey changed the list.

Jo
6

Tom put up his hand.
"I couldn't make the cookies," he said,
"because we didn't have any nuts.
I made some little pies instead."

Mrs Honey changed the list.

Paint
Red
Glue
MAGA
SCISS

Jim put up his hand.
"I couldn't make chocolate brownies," he said,
"because we didn't have any chocolate.
I made jam doughnuts instead."

Mrs Honey changed the list.

NER

Jo put up her hand.
“I couldn’t make the jam doughnuts,” she said,
“because we didn’t have any strawberry jam.
I made chocolate brownies instead.”

Mrs Honey changed the list.

Cass put up her hand.
"I couldn't make little pies," she said,
"because we didn't have any apples.
I made some cookies instead."

Mrs Honey changed the list.

NATURE CORNER

Kim put up his hand.
"I couldn't make toffee," he said,
"because we didn't have any vinegar.
I made a sponge cake instead."

Mrs Honey changed the list.

At the school fair,
Emma bought sponge cake.
Tom bought cookies.
Jim bought chocolate brownies.
Jo bought jam doughnuts.
Cass bought little pies.
And Kim bought toffee.

And Mrs Honey tore up the list.